Living LARGE

A Whale's Life

Sara Antill

PowerKiDS press.

New York

Published in 2012 by The Rosen Publishing Group, Inc.
29 East 21st Street, New York, NY 10010

First Edition

Editor: Jennifer Way
Book Design: Greg Tucker

Photo Credits: Cover, pp. 4, 6, 8, 10 (top, bottom), 11, 13 (top, bottom), 14 (bottom), 15 (left, right), 22 Shutterstock.com; p. 5 © www.iStockphoto.com/Josh Friedman; p. 7 © Minden Pictures/Masterfile; p. 11 © Franco Banfi/WaterF/age fotostock; p. 12 iStockphoto/Thinkstock; p. 14 (top) Jeff Hunter/Getty Images; p. 16 Mauricio Handler/Getty Images; p. 17 © www.iStockphoto.com/Chris Russick; pp. 18–19 Todd Bretl Photography/Getty Images; p. 20 Jason Isley-Scubazoo/Getty Images; p. 21 © www.iStockphoto.com/Earle Keatley.

Library of Congress Cataloging-in-Publication Data

Antill, Sara.
 A whale's life / by Sara Antill. — 1st ed.
    p. cm. — (Living large)
 Includes index.
 ISBN 978-1-4488-4978-9 (library binding) — ISBN 978-1-4488-5104-1 (pbk.) — ISBN 978-1-4488-5105-8 (6-pack)
 1. Whales—Life cycles—Juvenile literature. I. Title.
 QL737.C4A58 2012
 599.5—dc22
                                        2010049067

Manufactured in the United States of America

CPSIA Compliance Information: Batch #WS11PK: For Further Information contact Rosen Publishing, New York, New York at 1-800-237-9932

Contents

Biggest Animal in the World!

There are thousands of different kinds of animals in the world. Some, like ants, are very small. Others are very big. Have you ever wondered which animal is the world's biggest? The answer is the blue whale! There are many kinds of whales. Whales are some of the largest animals that have ever lived.

The orca, shown here, is also known as the killer whale.

This is a humpback whale. Humpbacks are found throughout most of the world's oceans.

Whales grow up to be very big. They start life much smaller, though. As whales get older, they grow, just as people do. The different stages of life that an animal passes through are called its **life cycle**. Let's learn more about the life cycle of a whale!

From Big to Bigger

Whales come in many different sizes. The dwarf sperm whale is the smallest whale. It is still a very big animal, though. Dwarf sperm whales can be as long as 8.5 feet (2.6 m) and weigh 600 pounds (272 kg).

The biggest whale is the blue whale. In fact, blue whales are the largest animals on Earth.

Adult humpback whales are about 48 feet (15 m) long and weigh around 40 tons (36 t).

The blue whale, shown here, is about twice as long and five times as heavy as a humpback whale!

A blue whale can grow to be 110 feet (33.5 m) long. It can weigh up to 150 tons (136 t). That is about as heavy as 75 cars!

Ocean Mammals

Whales live in oceans all around the world. They are not fish, though. Whales are **mammals**. This means they breathe air and are **warm-blooded**. Whales have a layer of fat under their skin called blubber. This keeps them warm. They can also live off the energy in the blubber when they are not eating.

This gray whale is coming to the surface to breathe.

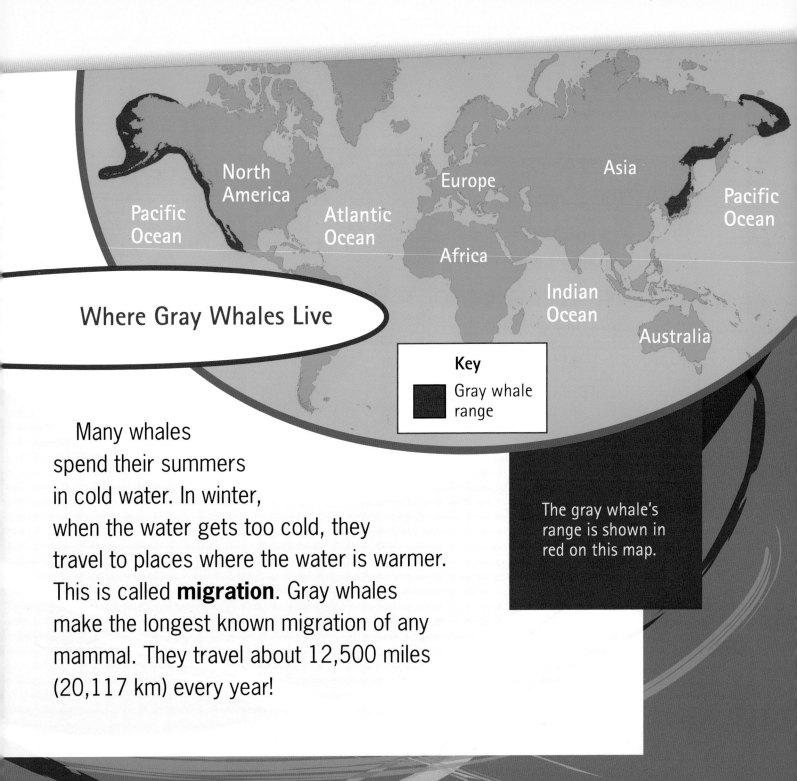

North America

Pacific Ocean

Atlantic Ocean

Europe

Asia

Africa

Pacific Ocean

Indian Ocean

Australia

Where Gray Whales Live

Key

Gray whale range

The gray whale's range is shown in red on this map.

Many whales spend their summers in cold water. In winter, when the water gets too cold, they travel to places where the water is warmer. This is called **migration**. Gray whales make the longest known migration of any mammal. They travel about 12,500 miles (20,117 km) every year!

Two Ways to Eat

There are two types of whales. These are toothed whales and **baleen** whales. Toothed whales have peglike teeth, which they use to catch their **prey**. They eat mostly fish and squid. They also eat other ocean mammals, such as seals.

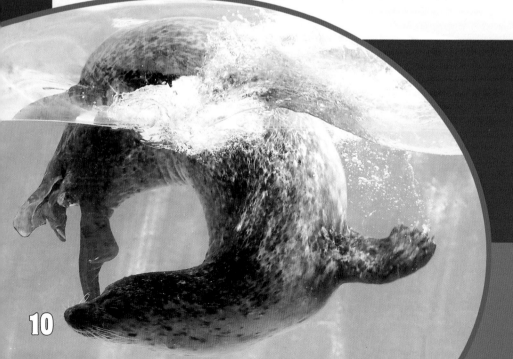

Top: Here you can see the baleen on this gray whale. *Left*: Toothed whales, such as orcas, prey on seals and other ocean animals.

Baleen whales feed very differently. Instead of teeth, they have hundreds of baleen plates in their mouths. These baleen plates act as filters. A whale can swim into a group of **plankton**, small fish, or **krill** with its mouth open. The small creatures will be trapped in the baleen plates, while the water is pushed back out the whale's mouth.

Sperm whales are toothed whales. They eat mostly squid.

11

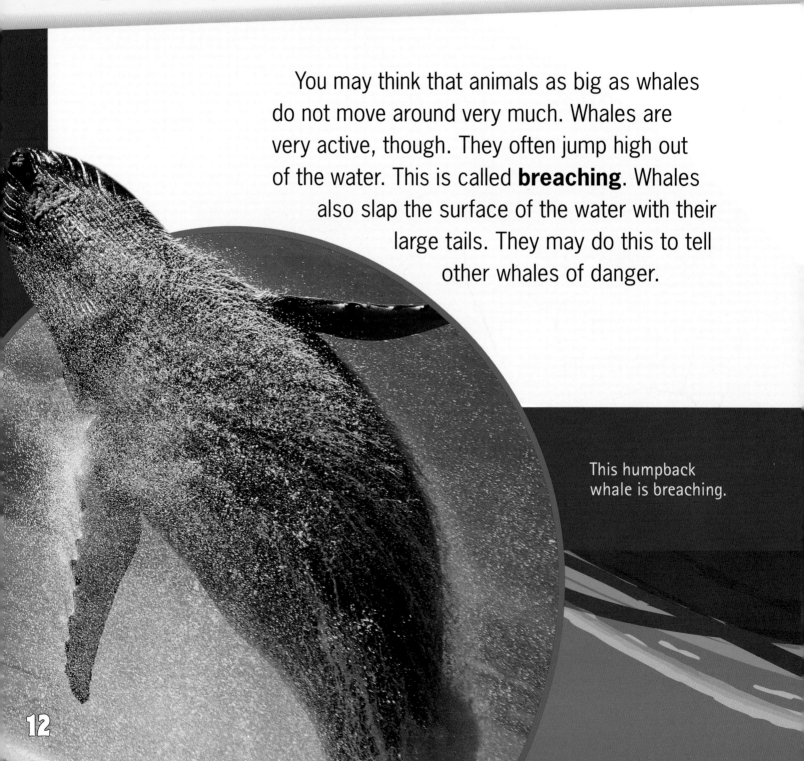

Jumping and Singing

You may think that animals as big as whales do not move around very much. Whales are very active, though. They often jump high out of the water. This is called **breaching**. Whales also slap the surface of the water with their large tails. They may do this to tell other whales of danger.

This humpback whale is breaching.

Right: Beluga whales are toothed whales. They talk to each other using whistles and clicks. *Below*: This humpback whale is slapping its tail on the water.

Baleen whales talk to each other using songs. These songs can be heard from many miles (km) away. They use these songs to keep track of each other. Toothed whales use whistles and clicks to find prey.

Life Cycle of a Whale

1 Baby whales, called calves, are born in warm waters. A calf will drink its mother's milk until it is one year old. A blue whale calf can drink as much as 200 pounds (91 kg) of milk every day!

4 Whales **mate** in warm waters. Between 9 and 16 months later, the female returns to the same warm waters to give birth. Females give birth to one calf at a time.

Young whales must learn from their mothers how to catch food. When they are about three years old, young male calves will leave their mothers and join a group of other young males. Female calves generally stay with other females until they are ready to mate.

2

Whales are fully grown between 6 and 13 years of age, depending on what type of whale they are. Most toothed whales live for around 30 years. Some baleen whales, such as the blue whale, can live much longer, up to 70 or 80 years.

3

Big Babies

Baby whales are called calves. A calf is born near the ocean's surface. As soon as it is born, its mother and other female whales will help lift the calf to the surface for its first breath.

When a calf is first born, it can weigh anywhere from 120 to 2,000 pounds (54–907 kg), depending on

Calves stick close to their mothers, as does the humpback calf shown here.

its **species**. A
newborn calf is generally
about one-quarter as long as its mother.
That means a killer whale calf can be
about 8.5 feet (2.6 m) long, while a blue
whale calf is closer to 23 feet (7 m) long!

Killer whales have calves
about once every five
years between the ages of
about 15 and 40.

Strong Bonds

Calves can swim very soon after they are born. As all mammals do, female whales nurse their calves with milk from their bodies. This milk has a lot of fat in it. This fat allows the young calf to grow very fast. In its first few weeks of life, the calf will double in size!

Mother whales have very strong bonds with their calves. Baleen whale calves will stay with their mothers until they are about one year old. Toothed whale calves will stay with their mothers even longer so they can learn how to catch prey.

This humpback whale calf will stay close to its mother for the first year of its life. Humpback calves can swim within the first half hour after being born!

19

Family Groups

By the time they reach 6 to 13 years old, young whales are full-grown adults. Some whales live in family pods, or groups. Other whales live in pods of all females or all males.

When a female whale is ready to mate, she will travel to warmer waters. There, male

Humpback whales travel and feed in groups. These groups generally break up after a few days, though.

whales, called bulls, will try to catch her attention. Once she has mated, the female will return to cooler waters for the summer. Between 9 and 16 months later, she will return to the warm waters once again to give birth.

Groups of humpback whales work together to trap fish by blowing bubbles in a small circle. This is called bubble-net feeding.

Whales in Danger

For many years, people hunted whales for their blubber. They used the blubber to make oil for lamps, candle wax, and soap. However, too much hunting caused many types of whales to become **endangered**.

Countries around the world have passed laws to stop people from killing whales. Some countries, though, still allow people to hunt whales. In Japan, whale hunting is allowed. The hunted whales are also studied. These studies give researchers new information not only about whales, but also about the ocean habitats in which they live.

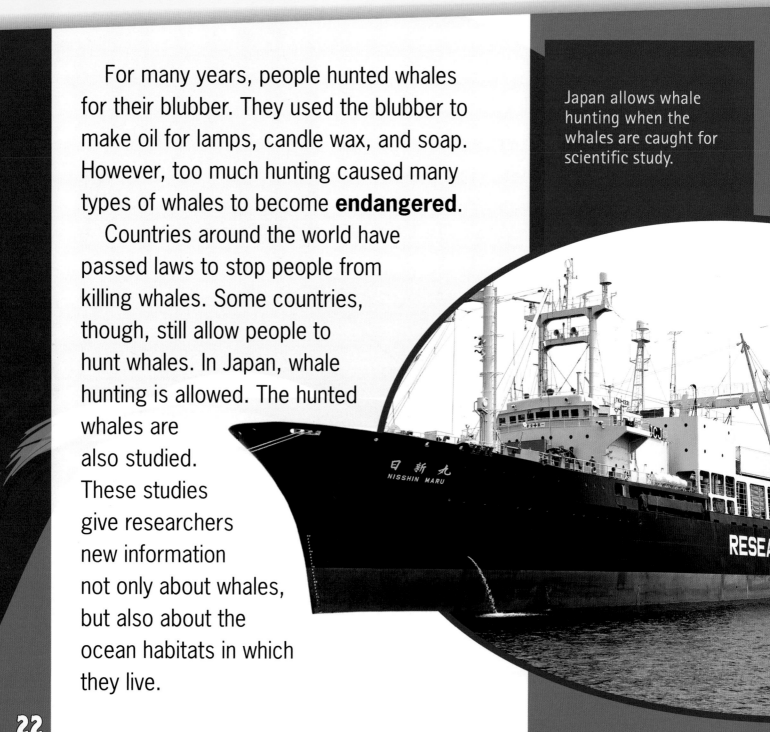

Japan allows whale hunting when the whales are caught for scientific study.

NISSHIN MARU

RESEA

Glossary

baleen (buh-LEEN) The structure through which baleen whales strain food.

breaching (BREECH-ing) Jumping out of the water.

endangered (in-DAYN-jerd) In danger of no longer living.

krill (KRIL) Tiny sea animals.

life cycle (LYF SY-kul) The different stages through which a living thing passes from birth to death.

mammals (MA-mulz) Warm-blooded animals that have a backbone and hair, breathe air, and feed milk to their young.

mate (MAYT) To come together to make babies.

migration (my-GRAY-shun) The movement of people or animals from one place to another.

plankton (PLANK-ten) Plants and animals that drift with water currents.

prey (PRAY) An animal that is hunted by another animal for food.

species (SPEE-sheez) One kind of living thing. All people are one species.

warm-blooded (WORM-bluh-did) Having a body heat that stays the same, no matter how warm or cold the surroundings are.

Index

A
ants, 4

B
blubber, 8, 22
breaching, 12

C
cars, 7

E
Earth, 6
energy, 8

F
fat, 8, 18

fish, 8, 10–11

K
kinds, 4
krill, 11

L
layer, 8
life cycle, 5

M
migration, 9

O
oceans, 8
oil, 22

P
people, 5, 22
plankton, 11
prey, 10, 13, 19

S
size(s), 6, 18
skin, 8
songs, 13
species, 17
squid, 10
summer(s), 9, 21

W
water(s), 9, 11–12,
    14, 20–21

Web Sites

Due to the changing nature of Internet links, PowerKids Press has developed an online list of Web sites related to the subject of this book. This site is updated regularly. Please use this link to access the list:
www.powerkidslinks.com/livl/whale/